Blueprint
to
Self Esteem
Middle
(School)
Girl Edition

"For we are God's Handiwork"
Ephesians 2:10

By Keisha Montfleury

I dedicate this book to ALL young girls:
For you to not only KNOW that you are GOD'S HANDIWORK!
But to also BELIEVE it!

This Book Belongs To:_____

Thank you for taking the time to read this journal!

Before we get started, there are 3 things that I want you to remember and take away from this book:

1. The most important relationship that you will ever have, is the one that you have with GOD! He will walk you through being the girl…and ultimately the young lady…that HE is wanting and needing you to become

2. The 2nd most important relationship that you will ever have, is the one that you have with YOURSELF. You should be caring for yourself, valuing yourself, and investing in yourself.

3. All of this takes PRACTICE! This is not something that happens overnight, you will have your good days, and your bad days, but PLEASE, PLEASE, PLEASE remember to NEVER GIVE UP ON YOURSELF!

Ok now that we got that out of the way, lets take a look at some things before we get started:

Do you know what SELF-ESTEEM means?

*It is the way someone feels about themselves

Someone can either have a high self-esteem or a low-self-esteem

I want you to think about YOUR self-esteem...is it high or low?

If you have a low self-esteem, I know EXACTLY how you feel, that is why I created this journal; so that we can PRACTICE the skills necessary to have a high self-esteem.

If you already have a high self-esteem, kudos to you!

Either way this journal will help us stay on track with making sure we are practicing having a high self-esteem

Now that you know what it means, I want you to write it down, so that you can remember it better.

Self Esteem is:

_____

_____

I want you to write it down 1 more time so that you can really remember!!

Self-Esteem is:

_____

_____

Ok 1 last thing before we get started, there are some important words that I would like you to remember because you will be seeing them thru-out this journal and they are very important:

Beautiful (Beauty-FULL; BeYOUtiful)- of very high standard; excellent (some synonyms are: graceful; elegant)
Ohh La La- YOUR "SHELL" IS YOUR OUTER BEING
Journey- to travel; to sail; to move from one place to another
Nourish- to provide with the food and other substances necessary for growth, health, and good condition
Investment- an act of devoting time, effort, or energy to someone or something with the expectation of a worthwhile result.
Intentional: done on purpose
Mindful: aware of something.

Beauty-FULL

Beautiful- of very high standard; excellent (some synonyms are: graceful; elegant)

Being BEAUTY-FULL is not only about what you look like on the outside, but it's a reflection of what type of person you are on the inside.
What type of person are you? Let's name at least 3 unique qualities that you have (just a reminder you HAVE something unique to offer the world)

1._____

2._____

3._____

Now I want you to write 3 affirmations (an affirmation is what something that you BELIEVE in yourself) …you will start each affirmation with the statement I AM (ex: beautiful, fun, an artist, unique)

1. I AM _____
2. I AM _____
3. I AM _____

*This is the PERFECT time to take a selfie and post it in the next page (take more pics with family and friends)

Place Selfie Here

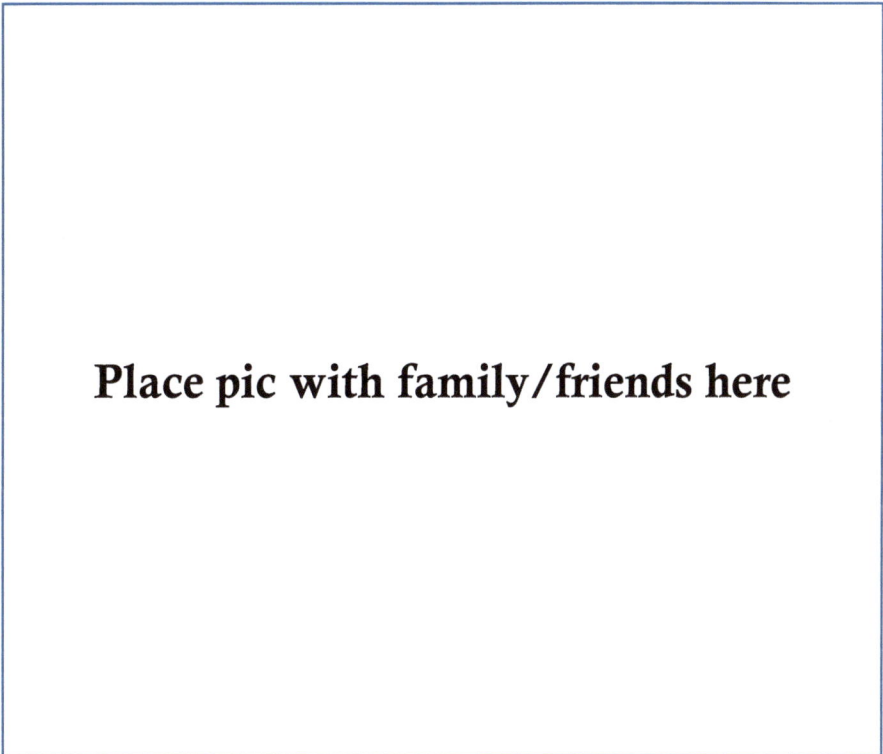

Place pic with family/friends here

Oooh La La, take a look at that girl!

*YOUR "SHELL" IS YOUR OUTER BEING

Hot tips for taking care of your shell

What's your skin type?

Oily

- Do you get a shiny nose and forehead?
- Is dry flaky skin something you know nothing about?
- Are you prone to blackheads and pimples?

Dry

- Does your skin feel tight after washing, even with the mildest of facial washes?
- Do you get itchy, flaky patches?

Combination

- Do you get a greasy forehead and nose but find your cheeks feel dry and tight?

Balanced

- Is your skin perfect- never dry and never oily? Well lucky you!

Now that you know your skin type let's see how to care for our skin:

✓ Cleanse- remember to rinse, rinse, rinse; pat your face dry with a lovely soft towel- don't rub it- your facial skin is very delicate and won't appreciate rough treatment

✓ Moisturize: moisturizer is like a protective layer, trapping in the skin's natural moisture and protecting against the buffeting your skin gets through the day from the sun, wind, and rain. You can apply your moisturizer after cleansing to your lovely skin. Just dab a little on your chin, forehead, nose and cheeks and rub it in gently until it disappears.

Other Tips for taking care of your shell:

✓ Take a bath/shower daily
✓ Comb/brush your hair (try new hairstyles) with your parents permission
✓ Moisturize your skin (i.e. lotion)
✓ Wear clean clothes (try new styles) get your parents permission

What are some other ways to take care of your shell?

✓ _____

✓ _____

✓ _____

*Check out and try the DIY recipes on the next couple of pages

Foaming Bath Soap

Ingredients:
1 cup sweet almond oil, (you may substitute a light olive oil)
½ cup honey, (local, organic honey is best)
½ cup liquid hand soap
1 tablespoon vanilla extract

Preparation:
In a medium bowl, add the oil and slowly stir in the remaining ingredients until fully incorporated. Pour mixture through a funnel into a clean plastic bottle with a squeeze top. Be sure to shake gently before using.

DIY Lipgloss

Ingredients:
Un-petroleum jelly
Coconut oil
Crystal light drink mix (various flavors)
Emergen-C

Preparation:
Step 1: Place about 1tsp of coconut oil and 1 tsp of un-petroleum jelly in a microwavable bowl. The amounts will depend on the size of the container you are putting it in. Place in microwave for about 60 seconds or until oil and jelly is melted

Step 2: Place powdered drink mix into the melted oil (about ½ tsp- 1tsp. or amount needed to get the desired color) Stir and stir until the mix dissolves. It may not totally dissolve and that is o.k. because as it sits in the container will it will dissolve some more.

Step 3: After it is pretty much dissolved pour it into your container.

Homemade Sugar Scrub

Ingredients:
2 ½ cups of sugar
¼ cup of baby oil
¼ cup of baby wash

Instructions:
Combine and mix ingredients in a bowl and then transfer to a jar,
For storage: use as an exfoliant for baby soft skin

These DIY's will get you started on taking care of your shell.

ENJOY!

Journey

(definition: to travel; to sail; to move from one place to another)

Do you notice that Journey is an action word? So that means a part of taking care of ourselves means we should make the time to exercise! Wait…. before you get overwhelmed or discouraged, or just plain old trying to tune me out, lets take a look at some of our options and see how easy it is get moving

(First, I want to let you know that exercising is not only good for your body, but also for your mind…it will help you start your day a little better, and help you to think more clearly, and help you feel better overall)

So there are 2 different types of Journey that I would like you to think about:
1.   Exercising your body
2.   Actually, traveling somewhere

OK!! SO LET'S START

If you could travel anywhere in the world, where would you go?
Write down 3 places you would love to visit

Another City

_____

Another State

_____

Another Country

_____

*Take the time to research these places
*Ask yourself "why do I want to go to these places"?
* Look up landmarks, and special places to visit
*Look up pictures, cut them out and paste them on the next page

Other City I Would Like To Visit (pictures, words to describe it)

Other State I Would Like To Visit (pictures, words to describe it)

Other Country I Would Like To Visit (pictures, words to describe it)

NOTES:

Fitness

Active Girl= Healthy Girl

Regular Exercising is important. In addition to helping your look and feel in shape, exercise strengthens you, gives you energy, helps you sleep better, makes your muscles stronger and more flexible, and build self-confidence.

So get up, and lets go!

Here are some ideas to get you started on exercising:

- ✓ Swim laps in the pool
- ✓ Ride a bike
- ✓ Do bleachers runs at your local highschool
- ✓ Play soccer or kickball in your backyard
- ✓ Shoot hoops in the driveway
- ✓ Hike a trail
- ✓ Sprints up and down your street
- ✓ Alternate between jumping ropes and jumping jax
- ✓ Play tennis
- ✓ Have a dance party
- ✓ Do trampoline tricks
- ✓ Roller skate (around your neighborhood; or at your local skating rink)
- ✓ Play Just Dance (or an active Wii game)
- ✓ Practice Yoga

My Work Out Schedule:

Days of the week that I choose to exercise (at least 3 days out of the week)

✓ _____ (Activity I will do…i.e walking, jogging)

✓ _____ (Activity I will do…i.e. playing Just Dance)

✓ _____(Activity I will do…i.e. skating, dancing)

How long am I going to work out? (at least 30 minutes each workout)

✓ _____

People I can ask to workout with me:

✓ _____

✓ _____

✓ _____

Nourish

Meaning: to provide with the food and other substances necessary for growth, health, and good condition

Being mindful of the things that you put in your body is another way that we can live a healthy lifestyle.

It can be a little challenging because you are not the one buying the groceries in the house; but there are many ways to get started on your new path.

1.   What is your favorite food to eat?

_____

2.   Does it remind you of something/someone?

_____

3.   Research the ingredients (what's in there?)

_____

4.   Can you change the ingredients around? Or add or take away something? Experiment with it and see what happens?

_____

*Below are ingredients for a breakfast dish, lunch dish, and dessert dish (check it out, try and make it, come on you can do it!)

The only kitchen equipment you will really need

Essentials: 10-inch nonstick skillet One good knife (a mini Santoku or sharp paring knife)

4-quart saucepan/pot

Cutting board 9X13-inch

aluminum pan Wooden or silicone spoon

Whisk

Flat spatula

Rubber spatula

Medium glass or metal mixing bowl

Measuring cups

Measuring spoons

2-cup liquid measuring cup

Can opener

Cheese grater

Hot pads

17

No Recipe Meals

Scrambled eggs or an omelet with ham and vegetables (zucchini, mushrooms, broccoli, etc.) Go crazy and add a side of whole grain toast.

Grilled or skillet-cooked chicken breast with steamed broccoli. Season both the chicken and broccoli well!

Panini (fancy name for a grilled sandwich). Here's a favorite: bread, deli turkey, sliced green apple (trust me), a little Dijon or regular mustard, and cheddar or swiss cheese.

Loaded quesadillas: take two tortillas and top one with any leftover chicken or steak (deli meat works great, too), cheese and any vegetables you like (you'd be surprised – almost anything is good on a quesadilla!). Toast in a skillet until golden and heated through.

Baked potatoes (regular or sweet potatoes). Top with chopped ham, sour cream, cheese – get creative!

Easy chicken parmesan. Sauté chicken (seasoned well with salt and pepper) in a skillet. When cooked through, pour in a cup or two of jarred spaghetti sauce, sprinkle shredded mozzarella over the top and serve over cooked pasta (or by itself!).

Healthier Chocolate No Bake Cookies

Makes 2-3 dozen cookies, depending on the size

- Ingredients 1 cup natural peanut or almond butter 1/2 cup

- coconut oil

- 1/2 cup honey

- 2 teaspoons vanilla extract

- 1 cup bittersweet chocolate chips

- 2 1/2 cups quick cooking or old-fashioned oats

- 3 tablespoons cocoa powder 1 cup coarsely chopped almonds (toasted is optional but awesome)

Directions

1. In a medium saucepan, melt the peanut or almond butter and coconut oil over medium heat, stirring constantly, until melted and smooth. Off the heat, stir in the honey and vanilla until combined.

2. Immediately stir in the chocolate chips until melted (if the mixture is too cool to melt them completely, return the saucepan to low heat to help it along without bringing it to a simmer).

3. Add the oats, cocoa powder and almonds and stir until well-combined.

4. Drop by heaping spoonfuls onto parchment-lined baking sheets or into a lined mini muffin tin. Refrigerate until set.

5. The cookies will keep in a tupperware-type container (layered between sheets of wax paper or parchment) in the refrigerator for a week or more.

Taco Bake

Ingredients

1

pound lean ground beef

1

medium onion, chopped (1/2 cup)

1

package (1 ounce) taco seasoning mix

1

can (16 ounces) tomato sauce

1

can (15.25 ounces) whole kernel corn, drained

2

cups shredded Cheddar or process American cheese (8 ounces)

2

cups Original Bisquick™ mix

1

cup milk

2eggs

Sour cream, chopped tomato and shredded lettuce, if desired

Investment

Investing in yourself and others is what we should strive to do

Be Intentional, Be Grateful, Be Mindful, Be YOU!!!

There are 2 ways that you can practice investing in yourself:

1.   Investing your time

2.   Investing your money

Investing your time means that you will need to make time for

YOURSELF

What are 3 things you like to do by yourself? (ex: read, draw)

_____

_____

_____

And for OTHERS (this can be parents, siblings, other family members, and friends)

Name 3 people you are going to spend more time with

_____

_____

_____

Another way to invest is by volunteering your time and money.

**You want to make sure you are being intentional = meaning you are going to invest in causes that you are passionate about or is of interest to you…(for example if you love pets or want to be a vet you might want to spend your time at an animal shelter; if you love kids, maybe you can volunteer at the local child care center) these are just examples

Name 3 places (or ideas) of places that you are interested in volunteering
_____
_____
_____

Name 3 places (or ideas) of places that you are interested in donating your allowance or money to

_____

_____

_____

A Note From The Author

Remember in the beginning of the book, we discussed 3 important things?

1. The most important relationship you will have is with

_____

2. The 2nd most important relationship you will have is the one you have with

_____

3. All of this takes

_____

BAMM!!! You got it! Now give me a hi-five!!
Ooops I forgot, I am not here!
Well…give yourself an air hi-five!!

**INTERNET
HIGH-FIVE
PLACE HAND
HERE**

There you go!

After reading through this book, my hope is that you are SUPER excited to do all the activities that will allow you to learn about yourself, and what it takes to practice having a positive self-esteem.

One other tip that I want to give you is to always REMEMBER to TALK TO GOD ABOUT EVERYTHING. Ask Him questions, seek HIS guidance, and listen to what He tells you about HOW to do these things. If you allow Him, He will let you know if various ways…maybe by bringing a new friend into your life, or bringing your and your mom closer, or allowing you to use your creativity to take care of your "shell".

Are you wondering how to talk to GOD?
Well I am glad you asked…BY PRAYING…it's that simple!! Praying is talking to GOD.

Below you will find a notes and prayers page, PLEASE use it, so you can write down your ideas, and your prayers.

Well I hope you enjoyed this journal, and hope that you will practice having a positive self-esteem! Because GIRL- YOU ARE WORTH IT!

Love,
Keisha

Prayers and Notes